The House in the Forest

I Talk You Talk Press

CONTENTS

CHAPTER ONE

Collette Roy looked through the window at the snow and trees outside. The sun was rising, and the sky was becoming lighter. She put her coat, hat and gloves on, and picked up her cup of coffee. She opened the door and sat on the step, enjoying the cold, fresh forest air.

My new life starts today, she thought.

Collette moved from Toronto to Overcreek last week. She liked Toronto, but she wanted to live in the countryside. When she lived in Toronto, she took the subway to work every day. The train was always full. She couldn't sit down on the train. There were many people in the city, and she always felt tired. She worked at a large elementary school. She liked the school, the teachers and the children, but she wanted to work at a smaller school in a smaller community. So she found a new job at Overcreek Elementary School. Overcreek was a very small town. Only 1,000 people lived there.

She found a nice house in Overcreek. The house was in the middle of a forest. It was a ten-minute drive from the house to the school. When the estate agent showed her the house, he said, "In summer, many people come camping near here, but in winter, no one comes. It's very quiet and lonely. It's not a good house for a woman living alone. How about an apartment in the town centre?"

"I like this house," said Collette. "It's quiet and peaceful. I left the city because I wanted to live in a quiet place. I'll take the house."

The estate agent was very surprised.

"Are you sure?" he said. "It's very lonely."

"Yes, I'm sure," said Collette. "I like it!"

There was only one other house near Collette's. It was in front of Collette's house, about fifteen metres away.

Collette drank her coffee and looked at the house in front of her. It was very old and dark. It was made of wood, and had a porch. It looked empty. There were no curtains on the windows, and there was nothing in the rooms.

It looks like it has been empty for a long time, thought Collette. *Why did the owners leave the house? Maybe they died. Or maybe they were old and wanted to live in the town centre.*

She finished her coffee and looked at her watch.

8:00am. Time to go to school! she thought. *I can't be late on my first day!*

Collette drove to school along the forest road. She was excited. She was looking forward to meeting all the teachers and children at her new school. She drove into the school car park. Some children were arriving early. When they saw Collette, they ran to her.

"Are you the new teacher?" they asked. "Where are you from?" "What's your name?" Collette laughed. "I'll tell you in class!" she said to them.

She walked into the school and went to the staff room. The other teachers were waiting for her. They were all very nice. They gave her a desk near the window. She looked out of the window at the town and the mountains behind.

The view is wonderful. I'm glad I came here, thought Collette. *I'm sure I'll enjoy working with these people. Everyone seems so nice and friendly.*

At lunch time, Collette was sitting in the staff room. She was talking to another teacher called Denise.

"Where do you live, Collette?" asked Denise.

"In the forest near the lake," said Collette.

Denise thought for a minute. "There are two houses near the lake. Do you live in one of those?"

"Yes, I do. I live in the newer one."

"Is the old one still empty?"

"Yes, it is."

"The children from this school don't like that house. They think that there is a ghost in the house!" said Denise, laughing.

"Well, the house looks scary," said Collette. "Especially at night. But I don't think there are any ghosts! Children have good imaginations!"

"That's true!" said Denise. "But some adults think that there is a ghost too."

"Really? Why?" asked Collette.

"Well, around twenty years ago, an old man died in that house," said Denise.

"How did he die?"

"He killed himself. He was very sad after his wife died. He didn't want to live anymore. Some people think his ghost still lives in that house. Oh, I'm sorry Collette. I don't want to scare you! I'm sure there is no ghost really!" said Denise.

Collette smiled. "Oh, it's OK. I don't believe in ghosts!"

Collette finished teaching at 3:00pm. Then she had to prepare everything for the next day. She finally finished work at 6:00pm. She enjoyed her first day at the school, but she was very tired. She got into her car and drove through the quiet streets to the supermarket. The sun was setting and the air was clear.

This is a beautiful place, she thought.

There was only one supermarket in the town. Collette spent a long time in the supermarket. Many people wanted to talk to her. She saw some children from the school with their parents. The cashier in the supermarket was very friendly. She asked Collette many questions about Toronto and her job. When Collette came out of the supermarket, it was dark. She looked at her watch.

It's nearly 8:00pm! she thought. *The people in this town like to talk!*

She drove through the dark forest to her house and parked her car. She looked across at the empty house.

It looks scary at night, she thought. *But I'm sure there's no ghost.*

She went into her house and locked the door. She closed the blinds and the curtains.

After dinner, Collette was very tired. She watched some TV programmes and went to bed early.

CHAPTER TWO

The next day, Collette was teaching her class. One of the boys said to her, "Ms Roy, where do you live?"

"I live in the forest near the lake," she said.

"Aah! Near the ghost house!" shouted the boy.

The other children started to talk excitedly.

"That's scary, Ms Roy! There's a ghost there! A real ghost!" said another boy.

Collette laughed. "There is no ghost!" she said.

"But there is! There is! Last summer, I went fishing on the lake with my older brother. We saw a shadow in the house. It was the shadow of a man!" said the boy.

"Yeah, I saw the shadow too!" said a girl.

"The ghost is really big and he sits at the window!" shouted the boy.

Collette shook her head. "No, there's no ghost! I live next to the house, and I have never seen any ghosts. The house is empty."

"But there is a ghost!" said the boy "I saw him! I did! I did! And he saw me! He looked at me!"

"OK! OK! Let's stop talking about the ghost. Let's do some reading," said Collette, opening the textbook.

These children really do have great imaginations, she thought.

Collette stayed at school until 8:00pm that night. She had a lot of paperwork to do.

When she finished, she got into her car and drove along the dark forest road. There were no lights along the road. The only lights were her headlights. They lit the road and the fir trees ahead on both sides of the road.

She turned off the main road and drove down the small road to the house. It was very icy, so she drove slowly. There was only one light between her house and the old, empty house. The light was like a city street light. It was very bright.

When she drove past the house, she looked at it.

"Oh!" she said.

She slowed down. There were footprints in the snow, from the road to the old house.

Maybe they are the footprints of an animal, she thought.

She stopped her car, rolled the window down and looked closely.

No, they are from boots, she thought. The footprints were deep and they led to the back door of the house.

Maybe the real estate agent went in, she thought. *Or maybe the local government did a check or something.*

She parked her car at the side of her house and went inside. She locked the door behind her. She pulled the blinds down on all the windows and switched on the lights. She made some dinner and then watched TV. Then, she went to bed.

CHAPTER THREE

The next morning, Collette woke up early. It was still dark. She went into the kitchen to make a cup of coffee. She looked out of the kitchen window and up at the dark blue sky.

I hope the weather will be nice today, she thought. She looked out across the forest. The light between her house and the empty house was shining brightly on the trees and the snow.

It didn't snow last night. Maybe spring is coming, she thought.

"That's strange," she said to herself. "The footprints…"

She opened the door. The early morning air was cold, but she didn't notice. She was looking at the snow through the trees. The footprints leading from the road to the other house were not there.

Maybe it did snow last night. Maybe new snow covered the footprints, she thought.

She looked up at the fir trees, but there was no new snow on the branches.

Collette closed the door and locked it.

Maybe I made a mistake last night. It was dark, she thought. *Maybe there were no footprints.*

She got her coffee from the kitchen and watched the news on TV while she got ready.

At 8:00am, she left the house.

When she drove past the empty house, she slowed down and looked carefully at the snow. There were no footprints.

Yeah, maybe I made a mistake, she thought. *But I'm sure I saw footprints…*

She drove into the school car park. She saw the real estate agent taking his daughter into the school. She parked her car and ran over to him.

"Good morning, Mr Harris!" said Collette.

"Good morning, Ms Roy!" he said. "How is the house? How is the school?"

"Everything is wonderful, thank you," said Collette.

"My daughter loves your lessons," he said. "She told me yesterday that you were talking about ghosts in class."

Collette laughed. "Yes, the children told me there was a ghost in the empty house."

The real estate agent smiled. "Yeah, all the children say that."

"Mr Harris, did you go to the old house yesterday?" she asked.

"No, I didn't. No one goes there. It's empty," he said. "Why?"

"Oh, no reason," said Collette.

Mr Harris looked at her. "Are you sure?"

"Well, last night, I saw footprints in the snow from the road to the old house," said Collette "But this morning, there were no footprints."

Mr Harris started to laugh. "I think the children scared you with ghost talk! Don't worry, there's no ghost. And the footprints? Well, I think it was the snow falling from the trees. That's all. You are from the city, Ms Roy. City people don't understand life in the countryside!"

Collette laughed. "I'm sure you're right!" she said, and walked into school.

CHAPTER FOUR

It was Saturday. Collette was very happy to have a day off. She was very tired, so she got up late, at around 11:00am.

She went to the kitchen to make a sandwich and some soup for lunch.

While she was heating the soup, she had a strange feeling. She went to the window and moved the blinds a little. She looked through the window blinds at the house. It was very sunny, and the snow was very bright.

"What was that?" Collette said to herself.

Through the trees, she could see a window of the empty house. She saw something move in the house. A shadow, crossing the room.

"Someone is in there," she said to herself. "Someone is in there."

She felt a little scared, so she moved to the side of the window and looked out through the side of the blinds. Nothing was moving.

Maybe I made a mistake, she thought. *Maybe it was the shadow of a tree moving in the wind. I shouldn't listen to the children's stories. I don't believe in ghosts.*

Collette went to her desk in the living room and sat down. She drank the soup. It was very quiet in the forest. The only sound was the melting snow dripping from the fir trees.

Crash!!

Collette screamed and jumped up from her chair. "What was that?!" she shouted.

She ran to the window and looked out at the empty house. She looked around the garden.

She saw a large block of ice on the ground. She sighed.

It was ice falling from the roof, she thought. *It's OK. It's only ice. Just ice.*

She went into the bedroom. The room was warm, so she opened the window a little. The air in the forest was very clear and fresh. She lay on the bed and soon fell asleep.

Collette woke up and looked at the clock. It was 4:00pm. She stretched her arms and yawned.

I need to get some food, she thought. *I'll go to the supermarket.*

She got into her car and drove down the road. She looked at the old house when she passed, but she didn't see anything strange.

Collette was driving back from the supermarket. She turned off the main road. Suddenly, her whole body felt cold.

Through the trees, she could see the door to the old house. It was open. She looked at the snow. There were footprints. They led from the door of the old house…to her door.

Collette's hands started to shake.

Oh no, she thought. *Someone is there. Someone is in my house.*

She drove off the road and into the forest. She parked her car between some trees. She got out of the car, and slowly and quietly walked towards her house.

She took out her mobile phone to call the police. Her hands were shaking.

Then, she noticed that the footprints continued around her house. Some of the footprints were big. Some were a little smaller. The snow was melting, so the footprints were not clear. She followed the footprints past the living room window, past the kitchen window and around to the back of the house. The footprints then continued into the forest. She looked around. She couldn't see anyone. The only sound was the wind blowing through the fir trees.

Maybe a family came walking in the forest, she thought. *But why did they come close to my house?*

Very slowly, she followed the footprints through the trees. She walked deeper into the forest. Soon, she came to the frozen lake. The footsteps stopped. She looked across the lake.

Did someone walk across the lake? she thought. Very carefully, she put one foot on the ice. It was very slippery.

No, this is too dangerous, she thought. *I will fall into the icy water.*

Collette looked around. There were no people, and no animals. Only the trees and the wind. She felt very alone.

I should go back, she thought. *I don't like it here alone.*

She walked back through the forest. The only sound was the snow under her shoes.

She stood in front of her front door and looked at the old house.

Is someone in there? she thought. She held her mobile phone tightly. *I'll look through the window. If I see someone, I can call the police.*

Slowly she started walking towards the house. She walked to a window. It was very dirty. She put her face to the glass and looked into the room.

The room was empty. There was no carpet and no furniture. The door was open. She could see into the hall of the house. It looked very dark. Collette shivered. She suddenly felt very scared. She ran back to her house. She put the key in the lock to open her front door. She tried to turn the key, but she could not turn it.

What? she thought. *What's wrong? Why can't I turn the key?* She started to panic. She turned the door handle. The door was unlocked.

Did I leave the door unlocked? she thought. *No, I always lock the door.*

She opened the door slowly and looked around. The house was very quiet. The only sound was the clock in the kitchen. She stepped into the house and closed the door behind her. She locked it.

Why is it so cold in here? she thought. She went into the bedroom and looked at the window. It was open.

Did I forget to close the window? she thought. She closed it and walked quickly through the house, checking all the windows and closing all the blinds and curtains.

She went into the living room and sat on the sofa. She was thinking about the window and the door.

A few minutes later, she heard a sound. There were voices!

She ran to the living room window and looked through the blinds. She could see a man and a young boy. She knew the young boy. He was in her class at school.

She opened the door.

"Hi, Simon!"

"Ms Roy! Hi!" said Simon. "Dad, this is Ms Roy, our new teacher," said Simon.

"Hi!" said Simon's dad. "We've just been for a walk in the forest. The air is very fresh at this time of year."

"Yeah," said Collette. "Did you walk past here?"

"We did, yeah," said Simon's dad. "Simon was a bad boy. He

opened the door of the empty house. I was surprised. The door wasn't locked."

"I opened the door because I saw the ghost! I wanted to catch him! But then I got scared. He was really big!" said Simon excitedly.

Simon's dad laughed. "Come on, let's get home. It's getting late."

"I looked through the window, Ms Roy. I saw a big man!" said Simon.

"Simon, you saw the shadow of a tree, that's all! Stop scaring Ms Roy!" said his dad.

"Ms Roy, is that your car?" asked Simon pointing to the car between the trees.

Collette looked at her car.

"Oh yeah, it is," said Collette.

"Why did you park there?" asked Simon.

"Oh, well, I er…" Collette didn't want to say 'I thought someone was in my house'. So she said, "I wanted to clear the ice from my parking space and garden."

"We can help," said Simon.

"No, it's OK. I can do it myself," said Collette.

Collette said goodbye and closed the door. Simon and his dad walked toward the main road.

She could hear Simon saying, "But I saw the ghost Dad! I saw him! He was a big man! He smiled at me!"

She waited for a few minutes then she went to her car and parked it next to her house. She took the shopping bags of groceries into the kitchen.

The footprints were Simon's and Simon's dad's, thought Collette. *Maybe Simon and his dad looked through my windows too. Maybe they came to my house to say hi.*

Collette unpacked the groceries and started to think about dinner.

I think I'll make pasta with tomato sauce, she thought. *I have a can of tomatoes.*

She took the pasta out of her bag. She opened the cupboard door and looked inside.

That's strange, she thought. *There are no cans of tomatoes. I bought a few cans at the supermarket the other day. Where are they? I thought I bought some cans of tuna too. Where are they?* She stared at the cupboard.

Collette closed the cupboard door.

I think I'm tired. Starting a new job is very stressful, she thought. *I left the window open, I forgot to lock the door, I didn't buy any cans of tomatoes. I didn't buy any tuna… I need a rest. I think I'll sleep all day tomorrow. At least I have milk and cheese.*

She made a cheese sauce for the pasta and ate her meal in the living room. At 9:00pm, she went to bed, but her bedroom was very cold.

That's because the bedroom window was open, she thought. *It will take a long time for the room to heat up again. I can't sleep in such a cold room.*

Collette remembered that she had a very thick, warm blanket.

Where did I put that blanket? I think I put it in the hall closet.

Collette went to the hall closet, but it wasn't there. She was very tired, so she gave up. She put a sweater on over her pyjamas. She took her thick winter coat from the closet and put it on the bed on top of her blankets. She climbed into bed and fell asleep.

CHAPTER FIVE

Spring came. Collette felt more relaxed. She was enjoying her job, and the weather was getting warmer. The snow melted and the forest was very green. People started to go to the lake. Many people put up tents and camped in the forest and on the shores of the lake. The days became longer, and on Saturdays and Sundays, Collette could hear the voices of children and families. They were camping next to the lake and in the forest. There were many cars driving along the forest road, and many people walking near her house every day.

One day, she was getting into her car when she heard some angry voices. She walked through the forest and saw two tents and two families. The families looked very angry.

"You took our food!" shouted a man.

"No we didn't! We have been walking in the forest! We haven't been near your tent!" said another man.

"You took cans of food from our tent! And you took our water!" shouted the man.

"Look in my tent! You will not find your cans of food or your water!" shouted the other man.

"Because you ate and drank it already!"

"Because we didn't take it!"

"I'm going to call the police!"

"Go ahead! Call the police! We didn't take your food!"

Collette didn't say anything. She walked back to her house.

Not happy campers! she thought. *But I wonder who took that family's food? There are many campers here. People go walking for many hours in the daytime. Anyone could take anything. I have to be careful too.*

The summer holidays came. More campers came to the forest. Some families stayed for a week or longer. Collette spent her days relaxing at her house. Sometimes, she went to the lake. The campers were very friendly. They talked to her and invited her to join their campfires in the evenings. They sat around the fire drinking and singing. She met people from many different places. She was having a very good summer.

Then, one night, everything changed.

Collette joined a campfire party down by the lake. She drank some wine at the party. She felt tired so she went back to her house and went to bed. She soon fell asleep. At about 3:00am, she woke up. She could hear strange noises. Then, she smelt something. Smoke!

Collette felt hot. She opened the curtains and looked outside. The forest was red and orange. There was thick grey smoke all around her house. The trees were on fire! She could hear people screaming. She ran through the house to the living room. Her house was full of smoke.

Crash!!!

She screamed. "What was that?" she shouted. She ran to the kitchen. A burning tree was falling into her kitchen! She tried to run to the front door, but it was blocked. The fire was starting to spread into the living room.

She ran back into the bedroom and banged on the window.

"Help! Help! Someone help me!"

She tried to open the window, but it would not open.

I must break the window! she thought. She looked around her bedroom. *What can I use to break the window?*

She started to panic. In her bedroom, there was only a bed and a closet. She looked out of the window. The fire was spreading. She couldn't see any people, but she could hear the campers' voices and screams from the forest. They were near their tents. No one could hear her, or help her.

I must escape! I must get out! she thought.

She ran to the living room again. She had to find something to break the window. Her sofa was on fire and the fire was spreading. There was heavy smoke in all the rooms. She couldn't breathe very well. She started to cough. She felt very weak. She ran to the window and screamed, "Help! Someone help me! I can't get out!" She banged on the window with her hands.

Then, she saw a shadow move in the empty house. It was a man. He ran out of the house and ran towards her.

Who is that? she thought. *It's a man. But I've never seen him before.*

"Help me! Help me please!" she shouted.

"Stand away from the window!" shouted the man. He was carrying a large stick.

Collette moved away from the window. The man smashed the window with the stick. Then, he reached into the room and grabbed Collette. He pulled her through the broken window. He was a strong man. He carried her past the old house and took her to the road. He put her down next to the road, away from the fire. Collette felt very dizzy. She couldn't see very well. She looked up at the man. She couldn't see his face because he was wearing a baseball cap. Collette could not speak. The man waited with her until he saw the flashing lights of the police cars, ambulances and fire engines. Then, he ran away into the forest. Collette lay on the ground and closed her eyes.

CHAPTER SIX

Collette was in hospital for a few days. She came out of hospital at the end of the summer holidays. She went back to school in September. All the children were still talking about the fire. The fire started with a camp fire. Some university students were camping. They got very drunk and fell asleep. The fire spread to the trees and through the forest. Luckily, no one died, but the fire destroyed Collette's house, her furniture, and everything else. The school found an apartment for her in the centre of the town.

The children wanted to know about Collette's escape.

"How did you get out of the house, Ms Roy?" asked Simon.

"Someone helped me," said Collette.

"Who?" asked Louis.

"I don't know his name. I think he was a camper," said Collette. She didn't want to tell the children about the man in the old house.

"What did he look like?" asked Louis.

"I couldn't see very well. It was very dark," said Collette. "And I felt very sick."

"How old was he?" asked Louis.

"I don't know! I couldn't see his face. But he was very strong. He picked me up and carried me to the road," said Collette.

"What was he wearing?" asked Louis.

"You ask a lot of questions!" said Collette.

"My dad is a policeman. He says questions are important," said Louis.

Collette laughed. "I see. Well, it was very dark, so I couldn't see very clearly. Maybe he was wearing pyjamas. It was late at night. Many people were asleep at that time."

"Was he young or old?" asked Louis.

"I don't know!" said Collette. "But I remember he had a tattoo on his wrist."

"The man saved your life," said Gina. "You have to say 'thank you'."

"Yes, Gina. You're right. He saved my life. He was very brave. I want to say 'thank you', but I can't, because I don't know where he lives and I don't know his name. I don't know anything about him. I hope I can see him again someday. I want to say 'thank you for saving my life'."

Later that night, Collette was watching TV in her new apartment in the centre of the town. The doorbell rang.

Who is that? she thought.

She opened the door. It was Louis' father, the policeman.

"Hi, Mr Lambert, said Collette.

"May I come in?" said Mr Lambert.

"Sure," said Collette. She took him into the living room and turned the TV off.

"Louis told me about the man who saved your life," said Mr Lambert.

"Yes, he was a very brave and kind man."

"Had you seen him before?"

"No, I had never seen him before," said Collette.

"Where did he come from?" asked Mr Lambert.

"I didn't tell the children this, but he came out of the empty house."

"Had you seen anyone there before?' asked Mr Lambert.

"No never. But sometimes that house was scary."

"Why was the house scary?" asked Mr Lambert

"Well, sometimes I saw shadows inside the house. They seemed to be moving. I thought they were the shadows of trees. Sometimes the sun was very bright and the trees in the forest are very big. But I never saw a person in the house, only shadows."

"Well, the fire destroyed most of the old house. But the old kitchen at the back of the house was built from stone. The fire didn't destroy the kitchen. We found nothing important. But we think someone was sleeping there. There was a very nice thick blanket and many empty food cans."

"What?" asked Collette. She suddenly felt very cold.

"Are you OK, Ms Roy?" asked Mr Lambert. "You look shocked."

"A blanket… What colour is it?"

"Purple. It looks quite new."

"I think it's my blanket. My friends at the school in Toronto gave it to me. It was a 'goodbye present'."

"Well, you say the man came out of the empty house. I think he was living there. I think he took your blanket." said Mr Lambert.

"How did he get into my house? I always locked my door."

"Did you ever leave a window open when you went out?"

"There was just one time. I opened a window. I forgot about it and I went to the supermarket. The house got cold. That night I looked for the blanket, but I couldn't find it."

"Did you notice anything strange about the house when you got back from the supermarket?"

Collette thought about that day. She remembered…the unlocked door…Simon…his dad…the footprints…the cold room…the cans of tuna and tomatoes…

"Yes, I did," she said. She told Mr Lambert about the footprints, Simon and his dad, the unlocked door and the missing cans of tomatoes and tuna.

"OK," said Mr Lambert. "I understand. The man was staying in the empty house. It was very cold and he had no food. He needed food and blankets. He saw you go out and he saw the open window. It was easy for him to climb through the window. He took your food and your blanket. Then he unlocked your door from the inside and walked out. I guess he was only in your house for about ten minutes. Why didn't you tell us? Why didn't you tell the police about the missing food?"

"It happened in my first week here. I was tired, and I thought I made a mistake," said Collette. "It only happened once."

"I understand. I guess you never left a window open again. We think he took food from the campers too. In spring and summer we had many calls from campers. They called us and said, 'Someone is taking our food and drink from our tents.'"

"I remember that. I saw two families fighting about food cans," said Collette. "When did he start living in the house?"

"Maybe you can tell me that. You moved into your house in mid-

March. The day you couldn't find the blanket and the food was missing, was the third weekend of March. Are you sure you didn't see or hear anything strange before that?"

"Just shadows in the house," said Collette. "No! Wait. There was one thing! The second day of school I saw footprints in the snow when I returned home after work.

"The footprints led from the road to the house. The next day, the footprints were not there. I thought that was very strange. I saw Mr Harris, the estate agent. I told him about the footprints. He said, 'It is snow falling from the trees.'"

Mr Lambert took a diary from his pocket and looked at it. "Yes!" he said. "I thought so! The second day after the school spring break was March 16th."

"Sorry," said Collette. "I don't understand."

"Well, on March 16th, a man stole some money from a shop in the town. Of course, everyone thought he left the area. But now, I think that he stayed close to Overcreek. I think he walked out to the forest to the empty house and stayed there. So you saw footprints that night. When you were asleep, I think he went outside and moved the snow with a branch to cover his footprints."

"How much money did he take from the store?"

"A few thousand dollars."

"But, who is he? Why was he staying in the house? I don't understand," said Collette.

"We think that the man was Noah Barker. He comes from Ottawa, but his wife lived in Overcreek when she was young. Many years ago, her grandparents lived in the old house in the forest."

"So, you think that Noah Barker stole the money and came to hide in the old house?" asked Collette.

"We are not sure. The storekeeper remembers that the robber had a tattoo on his left wrist. Noah Barker has a tattoo on his left wrist. He disappeared about the same time as the robbery. I went to talk to his wife. I asked her, 'Where is he? Where is Noah?' She said, 'I don't know'," said Mr Lambert.

"If Noah Barker took the money, why didn't he run away to Toronto or Ottawa?"

"He and his wife came to Overcreek in January this year. He got a job with a house building company. They rented a small house on the edge of the town. The house building company had money problems.

Noah worked for them for three months but they never paid him. The company always said, 'We will pay you next week', or 'We will pay you next month', but they never paid him. Then the company closed down and the owner went away. Noah had no job and no money. Mrs Barker was pregnant. They used all their savings in the bank while they were waiting for the building company to pay him. Then they had no money, and the building company didn't pay them. I think Noah Barker stole the money and then went to the empty house in the forest. I think he was waiting until the baby was born. Maybe his plan was to leave the area with his wife and the baby when it was born."

"So when was the baby born?" asked Collette.

"Mrs Barker had a son at the end of August. She seemed to have a little money. I asked her, 'Where did you get that money?' She said 'My mother is sending me money.' Then the day after the fire in the forest, Mrs Barker and the baby disappeared. No one knows where they went."

Mr Lambert looked at Collette. "Ms Roy, Louis said the man had a tattoo."

"Yes, that's right," said Collette.

"Where?"

"On his left wrist."

"What kind of tattoo?"

"I couldn't see very clearly. It was dark. Maybe a heart?"

Mr Lambert took a photograph out of his pocket. He passed it to Collette.

She looked at it. There was a man in the photograph. He had a tattoo on his left wrist.

"Was this the man?" asked Mr Lambert. "Did you see this man on the night of the fire? Did he help you?"

Collette looked at the picture for a long time. Then she looked at Mr Lambert.

She shook her head. "I don't know. I didn't see his face. It was dark and he was wearing a baseball cap."

"How about the tattoo? Is it the same design?"

Again, Collette shook her head. "I'm sorry Mr Lambert. I don't know."

"OK, I'm sorry to trouble you," said Mr Lambert, standing up. "If you remember anything about him, please call me."

"I will," said Collette.

"Goodnight Ms Roy."

"Goodnight Mr Lambert," said Collette. She watched him go down the apartment building steps, and closed the door.

CHAPTER SEVEN

It was nearly Christmas. Collette was back in Toronto for the Christmas holidays. She was shopping.

What can I buy my nephew, she thought. *He is five years old. Maybe he would like a train set.*

Collette walked into the toy shop. The shop was very busy. There were many children looking at the toys.

Collette found the train sets and picked one up.

This looks nice, she thought. *Joe will like this.*

She looked around. *Where should I pay?* she thought. Then, she saw the line of people waiting to pay. *The line is so long!* she thought. *Oh well, it is nearly Christmas. All the shops are busy.*

Collette joined the line. It moved very slowly. While she was waiting, she watched the other people in the shop. Then, a man and woman walked past her. The man was pushing a pram. Inside was a small baby. The man smiled at her when he walked past.

Who is he? Why is he smiling at me? she wondered.

The man and woman stopped to look at some toys. The woman pointed to a toy rabbit. It was on a high shelf. The man reached up to pick up the toy rabbit. As he reached up, Collette saw his wrists.

She was very shocked. The man had a tattoo on his left wrist.

I'm sure I have seen that tattoo before, thought Collette.

Is that him? she thought. *Is that the man?* She remembered Mr Lambert's story. The man's wife was pregnant. This man had a very young baby.

What should I do? Should I call Mr Lambert? Should I tell him about this man? thought Collette.

The man showed the rabbit to the woman. She looked at the price tag and shook her head. The man put the rabbit back on the shelf and the man and woman walked out of the shop.

It might not be the same man. I didn't see the tattoo clearly, thought Collette.

If it is the man who stole money from the store and stayed in the forest, I should tell Mr Lambert. But maybe it is not the same man. What should I do? The man in the forest saved my life. I should say 'thank you' to him.

"Next please!"

Collette jumped. The salesperson on the cash counter was waiting for her.

Collette paid for the train set. As she was walking out of the store she looked up at the rabbit on the shelf.

They looked like a nice young family. I don't think they have much money. Collette smiled to herself. *It wasn't the same man. I didn't see him in here. There is more than one way to thank someone,* she thought.

THANK YOU

Thank you for reading The House in the Forest! We hope you enjoyed the story. (Word count: 6,582)

There are quizzes about this book on our free study site I Talk You Talk Press EXTRA. http://italk-youtalk.com

If you would like to read more graded readers, please visit our website
http://www.italkyoutalk.com

Other Level 2 graded readers include
Adventure in Rome
Andre's Dream
A Passion for Music
Christmas Tales
Danger in Seattle
Don't Come Back
Finders Keepers…
Marcy's Bakery
Men's Konkatsu Tales
Salaryman Secrets!
Stories for Halloween
The Perfect Wedding
The School on Bolt Street
Train Travel

Trouble in Paris
Women's Konkatsu Tales

ABOUT THE AUTHOR

I Talk You Talk Press is a Japan-based publisher of language textbooks, graded readers and language learning/teaching resources.

Our team is made up of highly experienced language teachers and translators, who have all studied at least one additional language to an advanced level.

This experience enables us to design our materials from the perspective of both the teacher and the learner. We consult with both teachers and language learners when designing our textbooks and graded readers, and test our materials extensively in the classroom before publication.

We are a fast-growing press, and currently publish graded readers for learners of English. We publish new graded readers monthly.

www.ingramcontent.com/pod-product-compliance
Lightning Source LLC
Chambersburg PA
CBHW022351040426
42449CB00006B/829